AI in Education: An Educator's Handbook

Matthew Wemyss

This work is licensed under the Creative Commons Attribution 4.0

International License.

This means you are free to:

- Share, copy and redistribute the material in any medium or format
- Adapt, remix, transform and build upon the material for any purpose, except commercial reasons.

Under the following terms:

You must give appropriate credit to Matthew Wemyss (IN&ED) and indicate if changes were made. You may do so in any reasonable manner, but not in any way that suggests the licensor endorses you or your use.

Innovation & Education

Contents

Welcome   4

Part 1: AI in Education   7
   Chapter 1. The Current State of AI in Our Schools   9
   Chapter 2: Understanding Generative AI   12
   Chapter 3. Exploring the AI that's Out There   19

Part 2: Implementing AI in the Classroom   35
   Chapter 4: Mastering the Art of AI Prompting   37
   Chapter 5: Practical Applications in the Classroom   42
   Chapter 6. Ideas on How to Use Generative AI in the Classroom   50
   Chapter 7. The PAIR Framework for AI Integration   52

Part 3: Navigating Challenges and Building Partnerships   58
   Chapter 8: Addressing Challenges and Concerns   60
   Chapter 9. Engaging with EdTech and AI Companies   68

Part 4: Your AI Roadmap   73
   Chapter 10. Your School's AI Roadmap   75
   Chapter 11. Embracing the Future of Education   94

Appendix 1. Useful AI Tools   97

Welcome

Hi, I'm Matthew Wemyss a teacher, school leader, and proud father of two daughters.

Over the past 13 years, I've had the privilege of working in education across the UK and internationally, always striving to improve teaching and learning practices.

My journey with AI started as a personal tool to assist with my dyslexia. By using AI as a proofreader, I've been able to reduce the stress of creating error-free emails, letters, and lesson content. This initial exposure ignited my deeper interest in the possibilities AI holds for the education sector.

Lately, my focus has been on how AI is transforming classrooms—not just in the present, but also in terms of the future my daughters will grow up in. The impact AI will have on shaping their world is something we are only beginning to understand.

I co-host the Ctrl+Alt+Teach Podcast, and in July, I was honoured to receive the Edufuturists A.I. Pioneer award for my efforts in integrating AI into education. Additionally, I co-chair the COBIS ConnectED: AI/Digital Innovation sessions, where I help educators worldwide explore the evolving role of technology in schools.

For those interested in my work, you can find more on my blog and LinkedIn. I also highly recommend attending AIDUCATION at the Cambridge School of Bucharest, a fantastic CPD opportunity for anyone passionate about the role of AI in education.

The Promise of AI in Education

As William Gibson said, "The future is already here—it's just not evenly distributed." That's exactly what we're seeing with AI today. The tools are available, but many haven't yet realised just how accessible and powerful they can be in education. Generative AI is at our fingertips. We can use it in classrooms right now to simplify our work and, more importantly, improve how we teach. This isn't some far-off concept; it's a practical tool that can assist with everything from lesson planning to supporting personalising learning for our students.

What YOU Will Gain from This Guide

In this guide, I'll share insights from my experiences as a teacher, leader, and parent on how to effectively use AI in education. Here's what you can expect:

- Step-by-step instructions for using free, accessible AI tools
- Real examples from my classroom
- Tips to avoid common pitfalls (so you can skip the mistakes I've made)
- Practical advice on using AI ethically and responsibly

How to Use This Guide Effectively

This isn't a theoretical textbook—it's a practical guide, written by a teacher for teachers. Here's how to get the most out of it:

Start with the basics in Chapters 1 and 2. Even if you're tech-savvy, don't skip them—AI might work differently than you expect.

Test out one tool or technique at a time. No need to overhaul everything at once.

Use the reflection questions at the end of each chapter to adapt ideas to your own classroom.

Share your experiences with your colleagues—AI is a new learning curve for everyone.

This guide isn't about replacing teachers with AI bots. It's about using AI to enhance the things we already do well.

Ready to make AI work for you and your students? Let's get started.

Part 1: AI in Education

Chapter 1. The Current State of AI in Our Schools

Let's be honest about where we are:

- Many of us are still getting to grips with basic edtech.
- Our students are often more tech-savvy than we are.
- We're curious about AI, but we're cautious about the hype.

The good news? You don't need to be a computer scientist to start using AI effectively in your classroom. In fact, you're probably already using some form of AI without even realising it. Ever used predictive text or autocorrect? That's AI. How about Google Translate for EAL students? Yep, AI again.

Challenges and Opportunities

The potential for AI in education is enormous, but integrating it comes with challenges:

- **Ethical Use:** How can we ensure that AI is used in ways that respect student privacy and promote fairness? What precautions should we take when considering AI for high-stakes assessments or handling sensitive data?
- **Equitable Access:** How do we prevent AI from increasing the divide between students with access to technology and those without? Similarly, how can we address the disparities between schools with the necessary infrastructure and those lacking it?
- **Maintaining the Human Element:** While AI can enhance teaching, how do we ensure it doesn't diminish the empathy and personal connection that only great teachers can offer?

But with these challenges come opportunities. Opportunities to discuss these challenges with our students. As AI continues to progress, they will have to grapple with them into their adult lives.

We will explore these issues further in Chapter 8, focusing on the potential for AI in education, how we can address these challenges.

How AI is Changing the Educational Landscape

We've called AI's impact on education everything from a disruption to a revolution, even an evolution. With so many buzzwords, it's no wonder people are confused. Are we talking about a radical transformation of the classroom, or just a gradual shift? The constant rebranding makes it hard to see what's really happening and what's at stake.

The changes are here, whether we notice them or not. A private school in London is about to open the UK's first AI-led classroom, claiming AI can deliver personalised, precise lessons better than any human. Alpha School in Austin is expanding its AI-driven curriculum to offer bespoke learning experiences. The headlines might suggest teachers are being replaced, but the reality is different; they're still there, just rebranded as "guides."

There's also a growing assumption that students instinctively know how to use AI, but this isn't always the case. Some students adapt quickly, of course, but not all. We're already seeing gaps in AI literacy, and that's something we can't afford to overlook.

Studies show that unchecked use of tools like ChatGPT can stifle deep learning, but when AI is thoughtfully integrated, especially with teachers guiding the process, it can enhance education by providing personalised feedback and support that humans alone can't match.

What if these approaches turn out to be wildly successful? The impact could be enormous. Education could become more adaptable and responsive to individual needs, or it could become reliant on screens.

The real question isn't whether AI will enter classrooms...it already has. The question is, how far will it go?
We're at a pivotal moment. The good news is that it's not too late to start your own AI journey. Don't worry about catching up all at once; the key is to begin.

Now let's focus on real ways AI can impact classrooms today. The future of education is being shaped now, and it's up to us to shape it wisely.

Chapter 2: Understanding Generative AI

What is Generative AI?

Think of Generative AI as a super-intelligent assistant that can write, draw, or even code based on your instructions. It's not just a tool for analysing or categorising data—it can actually create new content.

You give it a prompt, and it generates text, images, or code based on what it has learned from a huge amount of data. It's like working with a personal assistant who has read every book and can recall all that information instantly.

In the classroom, this means we can use Generative AI to:

- Create quiz questions
- Develop real-world scenarios or problems for students to solve
- Produce images to inspire creative writing

However, while it might seem impressive, it's important to understand that Generative AI doesn't truly "understand" like humans do. It's great at identifying patterns, but it's not sentient.

What Generative AI is and What it is Not

Generative AI is a subset of machine learning that uses deep learning, a method where computers learn from huge amounts of data, like how humans learn from experience.

But unlike regular machine learning systems that just predict or suggest things based on patterns, Generative AI can actually create based on your input.

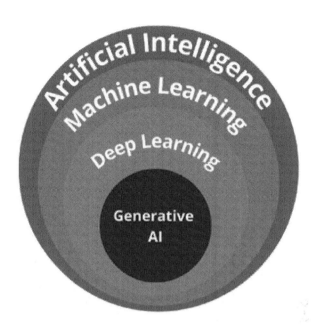

Let's break down the layers in this diagram:

- **Artificial Intelligence (AI)** is the big picture, covering everything that involves a computer doing tasks that usually need human intelligence, like recognising speech or making decisions.
- Inside AI, we have **Machine Learning**. This is where the computer learns from examples. Think of it like a student getting better at solving maths problems by practising over and over, recognising patterns, and figuring out how to improve.
- Going deeper, we get to **Deep Learning**. This is a more advanced version of machine learning. Imagine a computer using a really powerful learning system, similar to how our brains work, to handle huge amounts of information and learn from it in a more detailed way.

- Finally, at the centre, there's **Generative AI**. This is the most creative layer. While regular AI might just suggest something like "What movie should you watch next?" Generative AI can do much more. It can actually *create* something, whether it's writing a story, drawing a picture, or even composing music, all based on what you ask it to do.

In short, AI helps computers think and learn. Generative AI is the special bit that gives them the ability to *create*.

What Generative AI is

Text Generator: It can write stories, essays, or any other form of written work based on a prompt.
Example: *You ask for a story about a detective, and it creates a unique narrative from scratch.*

Artistic Creator: It generates new images, illustrations, or even music based on a description.
Example: *You describe a futuristic city, and it produces a brand-new digital artwork.*

Code Writer: It can write new code to solve problems or create apps.
Example: *You request a Python script for a basic game, and it produces usable code.*

What Generative AI is Not

Recommendation System: It doesn't just predict what you might like based on patterns, like Netflix or Spotify does with their recommendations.

Autocorrect: It doesn't just fix typos or suggest the next word. Generative AI creates a whole paragraphs based on your input.

Voice Assistants: It goes beyond Siri or Alexa setting reminders or giving weather updates. Generative AI can engage in complex conversations and even create original stories or articles on demand.

Learning Platforms: It's not just serving up pre-programmed answers or multiple-choice quizzes like some e-learning systems. Generative AI can engage in back-and-forth dialogue, explain complex topics in various ways, and even create custom learning materials on the fly.

So, while tools like Netflix, autocorrect, or traditional learning platforms use machine learning to make predictions or suggestions based on past data, Generative AI, powered by deep learning, goes much further by creating new content from scratch, based entirely on your instructions.

It's not just pulling from a database of pre-written responses; it's crafting unique content in real-time!

Key Concepts (in plain English)

To use Generative AI, it's helpful to understand some basic terms:

Term	Definition
Artificial Intelligence (AI)	The idea of machines doing things that usually need human intelligence, like learning, problem-solving, or making decisions.
Machine Learning	A type of AI where machines learn from data and get better at tasks over time, without needing to be told exactly what to do.

Deep Learning	A more advanced form of machine learning where the AI learns from huge amounts of data, similar to how the human brain works (a neural network).
Neural Networks	The system AI uses to process information, inspired by the human brain. It's made up of layers that pass data between "neurons," helping the AI learn patterns, make decisions, and solve problems.
LLM (Large Language Model)	The "brain" of a generative AI system, trained on massive amounts of text so it can create human-like responses.
Training Data	The large amount of information (like text, images, or code) that AI uses to learn how to respond to different requests.
GPT (Generative Pre-trained Transformer)	A type of AI model designed to generate human-like text based on prompts it receives. It's one of the most popular types of generative AI.

Prompt	The instruction you give to the AI, telling it what to do. The clearer and more detailed your prompt, the better the AI's response.
Inference	This is the step where the AI takes your prompt and uses patterns it learned during training to create a response.
Tokens	Small pieces of text (words or parts of words) that the AI breaks input into. AI tools often have limits on how many tokens they can handle at once.

Understanding and Using Generative AI

Curious about how generative AI works? A great place to start is by asking an AI itself. Tools like ChatGPT can break down complex concepts in simple terms.

Try prompting it with, "Can you explain generative AI like I'm 5?" This will give you an easy-to-understand overview, and from there, you can ask for more detailed explanations.

This process mirrors the "learning pit"—where initial confusion leads to deeper understanding through questioning.

So, as you engage with AI, pause whenever something doesn't make sense and ask follow-up questions until everything clicks.

And here's the catch—AI is biased

Why? Because the data it learns from often carries the biases of the real world—whether those biases are cultural, historical, or related to perspectives that have been more widely represented. If the AI's training data is skewed toward a particular viewpoint, the output it generates may reflect those same biases.

You can also prompt the AI to consider more diverse perspectives. For example, ask it to provide alternative viewpoints or include insights from underrepresented groups in history, literature, or any subject you're teaching.

AI as a Creative Partner, Not a Shortcut

The true value of AI isn't in simply churning out lesson plans with the push of a button. Its strength lies in acting as a creative collaborator. AI has "seen" thousands of lesson plans, activities, and strategies, and when you need support, it can tap into that vast knowledge.

However, it's crucial to remember that AI works by generating responses based on patterns in data. If you're after something conventional, AI will give you the most likely, predictable version of that lesson plan, email or activity.

But if you're aiming for innovation, something that breaks away from the norm, you'll need to guide the AI and make the final creative leap yourself.

This is where the art of prompting comes in Chapter 4. With well-crafted prompts, you can steer AI toward more creative, tailored, and relevant outcomes. Think of AI as a tool to ignite your ideas...a starting point, not the endgame.

While it can kickstart the process and generate possibilities. The real creativity, innovation, and final decisions rest firmly in your hands.

Chapter 3. Exploring the AI that's Out There

As educators, we're always on the lookout for tools that can make our lives easier and our teaching more effective. Now let's look at some specific AI tools. This isn't an exhaustive list – I'm focusing on the ones I have used and do use alongside tools like ChatGPT etc. You'll find a longer list of tools in Appendix 1.

Meeting Transcription

Otter.ai transcribes meetings. It connects with Zoom, Microsoft Teams, and Google Meet, automatically recording conversations and generating real-time transcripts, action items, and summaries.

Video Generation

Platforms like **Leonardo.ai** and **Runway** are simplifying video creation. Leonardo.ai provides 150 images per day on its free plan, perfect for creating educational content, while Runway offers an initial 125 credits before switching to a paid service. Both are useful for generating visual aids or short video clips for lessons

Text-to-Speech

Eleven Labs is a great tool for converting text into lifelike speech, offering voice cloning and text-to-speech features. The free plan is great for creating podcasts or audiobooks for students, or for bringing a bit of flair to presentations with realistic AI-generated voices.

AI Search Engines

Perplexity is an AI-powered search engine that doesn't just provide results—it backs them up with references and citations. It's the perfect mix of using Generative AI and having reliable, traceable sources for research projects or lesson planning.

Image Generators

Bing Image Creator is free for Microsoft users, while **Midjourney** offers more sophisticated options with a subscription. **NewArc** is a standout for art, and Design and Technology teachers with its free educational accounts, allowing students and educators to create stunning 3D renders and visuals.

Creation and Publishing

Canva continues to be a teacher's best friend, offering its full suite of creative tools for free through the education license. Teachers get access to AI-powered design and publishing features, while students can use it to create everything from visuals to presentations (students cannot use the AI writing tools that teachers can access).

Music Creation

Suno and **Udio** offer free plans with daily or monthly limits. Suno allows up to five songs a day, and Udio provides 10 credits, each generating 30 seconds of music. Both are useful for quickly creating background tracks or audio content for educational projects.

AI-Powered Websites for Teachers

A variety of platforms like **SchoolAI**, **Magic School**, **TeachmateAI**, **TeacherMatic**, and even **Quizizz** now offer AI-driven tools designed for teachers. These platforms provide features like lesson planning, worksheet creation, and quiz generation, essentially acting as 'wrappers' on top of existing AI models like ChatGPT.

While I personally prefer training teachers on how to prompt AI directly, I do see the appeal of these tools. They provide user-friendly interfaces, making AI more accessible to educators, providing an entry-level into generative AI.

My AI in Education Usefulness Scale

This is a personal guide based on my own experiences with various AI tools in the classroom. From text generation to song creation, I've ranked these tools from "high" to "low" in terms of their usefulness and impact on my teaching. While this scale reflects my individual journey, it's not meant to offend or dismiss other tools that I might not have explored yet. I am certain there are many more platforms out there that offer great value.

That said, this guide serves as a reference to help you start your own exploration and make informed decisions about integrating AI into your practice based on what I've found to be effective.

High

Text Generation	I use tools like ChatGPT, Gemini, Co-pilot, and Claude every day for tasks like lesson planning, creating resources, proofreading, and reviewing emails or letters. They're especially useful for improving clarity or adjusting the tone of emails. These tools also help with coding projects, such as building websites or custom games for students.
Creation and Publishing	I use Canva daily, and its AI features are a huge time-saver. The magic tools are especially helpful for teachers. You can also try other AI presentation generators like Gamma, though many of these are freemium or paid options (check the appendix for more suggestions).
AI Search Engines	As an educator, I use Perplexity for lesson planning and research, and I find it helpful that it provides references with its AI responses. Microsoft Copilot (for Office365 schools) does the same, making both tools useful for accuracy and transparency.

	Medium
Image Generation	While some platforms offer free image generation, the quality tends to be lower than paid versions. Image generation supports literacy development (using descriptive words), and our English and Drama teachers use it to create custom images for creative writing and performance inspiration. NewArc could be placed in high for subjects like Art and D&T. It is great for visualising prototypes, and different types of material.
Text-to-Speech and Voice Cloning	I've combined text and speech generation to create custom podcasts for my students, making this a useful tool for personalised learning.
AI-Powered Websites for Teachers	Platforms like Quizizz, which I use for retrieval practice, have useful features like generating quizzes from lesson content. However, using them too much can reduce their impact. In general, AI-powered teacher websites can be a good starting point, though I prefer creating my own prompts. My school is also trying out AI tools for students (see the Edubots section of this chapter). I believe it's better to use a "wrapper" or third-party platform for these, mainly for security and peace of mind. I prefer a platform where I can monitor and access students' interactions with the AI bots I create.

Low

Video and Song Generation

Personally, I haven't found any strong uses cases of these AI tools specifically for my subject, computer science.

While there are some potential applications for the creative arts. These tools can be fun, but they haven't shown much impact in improving understanding. Video creation tools, in particular, are mostly paid and still developing. The idea of making custom visuals and audio for lessons is exciting, but I feel the technology isn't quite ready to meet classroom needs...yet.

Transcription

Since I work with students under 18, who have restricted access to many AI tools due to terms and conditions, these tools have had a low impact on my classroom practice so far. However, their usefulness could be rated as medium, as they do save time by automating tasks like converting lecture notes into flashcards or other study aids, which some university-age students find beneficial.

I do use these tools occasionally in meetings, but it does irk me when an AI transcriber arrives solo.

Bonus Tool: Google's NotebookLM

NotebookLM is an AI-powered note-taking app from Google that helps users organise and process information from various sources.
Here's a quick summary of the features I find useful:

- **Quick Access to Documents:** Easily store and retrieve course materials, saving time when preparing lessons.
- **Private and Secure:** Since it's private, I can review sensitive documents like policies without data-sharing concerns.
- **AI Responses from Uploaded Documents**: The AI only uses my uploaded materials, ensuring accurate and relevant answers.

I've also been testing the **Audio Overview** feature for creating podcast-style summaries for students.

Edubots for Students (Student-Facing AI)

While 99% of our current AI use is focused on staff training and helping teachers become proficient in using AI tools, we're now beginning to explore student-facing AI through EduBots.

"What's an EduBot?" I hear you ask. An EduBot is an AI-driven chatbot designed to assist students with specific tasks, like answering questions, offering additional support, or tutoring.

These bots come with clear instructions and are purposefully focused on a single area to enhance learning in a structured way.

However, before diving into student-facing AI, I believe it's crucial for schools to first get teachers comfortable with prompting and using AI.

Once educators have a solid understanding, transitioning to tools like EduBots becomes a manageable next step.
Key considerations when implementing EduBots include how students will access the bot (whether they need accounts or it's open access) and how their interactions will be monitored. I prefer platforms with teacher dashboards for monitoring usage and ensuring safeguarding.

Two platforms I've found effective are SchoolAI and Mindjoy. They offer easy deployment of EduBots and comprehensive dashboards for overseeing student interactions, ensuring a safe and monitored environment.

Edubot Examples

Here are some examples of EduBots I've used with students, all grounded in sound pedagogical principles. Each bot has a specific purpose, from tutoring to providing additional support, ensuring students stay focused and engaged. They're all hosted on Mindjoy, but you can create a free account and access the prompts yourself. Use the QR codes to access each of the Edubots.

Bot 1: The Why Wanderer

This Edubot was one of the first I built for students, and I'm proud of it. It uses the "5 Whys" technique to encourage deeper thinking by asking "why" repeatedly, helping students get to the root of a problem and think more critically.

Bot 2: Rosenguide

This bot is built on Rosenshine's Principles of Instruction, which focus on effective teaching strategies. I've used it as the foundation for the in-class tutoring bots that support my students, helping them reinforce their learning and improve their understanding in real time.

Bot 3: RockyBitboa

This bot is built around coaching best practices. After an assessment, students use it to focus on their areas for improvement, providing them with tailored support and guidance to help them progress.

Bot 4: Adabot

This coding support bot offers guidance without giving away the answers. It helps students work through problems on their own, which is a big help when I'm managing a class of 20+ students learning to code.

The AI-lephant in the Room

When exploring AI tools, it's easy to get caught up in the excitement they generate. However, there's an often-overlooked issue that every educator must confront—the terms and conditions of these platforms. This 'AI-lephant in the room' can be a significant hurdle, especially when it comes to student use.

Many AI platforms have strict age-related terms of service that limit access for younger users. These restrictions typically fall into the following categories:

> **Under 13:** Not permitted to use the platform.
> **Ages 13 to 18:** Permitted with parental consent.
> **18+:** Full access without restrictions.

Integrating AI into classrooms can be challenging, especially with younger students. Schools may hesitate due to the need for parental permission and the complexity of enforcing age restrictions.

To manage this, we're exploring AI platforms that meet legal requirements while offering valuable learning experiences for students between the ages of 13 to 18. It's a careful balance between staying compliant and giving students meaningful access to AI tools.

At the time of writing, I'm not aware of any schools that have fully adopted a system of seeking parental permission for AI use on a broad scale.

However, I strongly recommend keeping parents informed about how AI is being used in school. Transparency helps avoid misunderstandings and reassures parents, preventing unnecessary concern.

The Golden Rule: Try It Yourself

Here's the most important thing I've learned about AI tools: the only way to really understand what they can do is to experiment with them yourself. What works brilliantly in one context might fall flat in another.
I encourage you to adopt a 'try it and see' approach.
Start with low-stakes tasks – maybe use AI to help plan a single lesson or to generate some discussion questions. See what works for you and your students.

AI in Education: Time to Take Action

Now that you've worked through Part 1 and explored the current state of AI in our schools, it's time to move from theory to practice. This exercise is designed to help you reflect on what you've learned and, more importantly, start applying it straight away.

So, let's dive in. Fill out the self-assessment, pick your first action, and begin the journey to making AI a meaningful part of your classroom. Ready? Let's go.

Step 1: Self-Assessment

Rate your level of agreement with the following statements on a scale of 1 to 5:

1 = Strongly Disagree
2 = Disagree
3 = Neutral
4 = Agree
5 = Strongly Agree

Statement	Score
I can confidently explain Generative AI to my colleagues.	
I'm comfortable with key AI terminology (e.g., prompts, tokens).	
I can identify AI tools that would benefit my teaching.	
I understand why protecting student data is crucial when using AI tools.	
I can spot and address potential biases in AI-generated content.	
I can think of ways AI can support my lesson planning.	
I am aware of the hurdles in bringing AI into the classroom.	
I feel prepared to evaluate AI tools for their educational value.	
I feel confident about implementing AI to support my teaching	

Score Summary

Once you've completed the scorecard, add up your scores to see where you are on your AI journey. Remember, this is just a guide to help you move forward!

40-45: AI Pioneer! You're ready to lead the way in AI integration. Share your insights and mentor others—you have the skills to inspire your colleagues.

30-39: AI Enthusiast! You've built a strong foundation, and now it's time to dive deeper into new AI tools and techniques. Keep up the great work!

20-29: AI Explorer! You're making fantastic progress. Continue experimenting with AI, and you'll soon see even more impact in your classroom.

9-19: AI Beginner! Every journey starts with a single step. Focus on learning one or two key AI tools and watch your confidence grow from there.

No matter where you are on the scale, remember that AI is an evolving field. Every score represents an opportunity to grow, explore, and make AI a meaningful part of your teaching practice. You've got this!

Step 2: Set Your Post-Part 1 Action

Now, it's time to act! Reflect on what resonated most with you and choose one concrete action to take next. This will help you turn theory into practice.

What's the one thing you will do after completing Part 1?

Write it here:

Part 1 Recap

In Part 1, we've taken a deep dive into the current landscape of AI in education. We've explored the state of AI in our schools, demystified Generative AI, and looked at some practical AI tools that are ready for classroom use. This section has laid the groundwork for understanding how AI is reshaping education and the potential it holds for enhancing our teaching practices.

Key Takeaways:
1. AI in education isn't some far-off sci-fi dream; it's here, and it's ready for us to use.
2. Generative AI acts like an assistant, not a replacement for teachers.
3. There's a wide range of AI tools available, from text generators to image creators, each with different applications in education.
4. Understanding the basics of how AI works helps us use it more effectively and ethically.
5. The integration of AI in schools varies widely, but there's room for everyone to start their AI journey.

Next Steps:

1. Reflect on your current use of technology in the classroom. Where might AI fit in?
2. Choose one AI tool from Chapter 3 to explore further. Start small - maybe use it to help plan a single lesson or generate some discussion questions.
3. Familiarise yourself with key AI terminology. Understanding terms like 'prompts' and 'tokens' will help you navigate AI tools more confidently.
4. Consider the ethical implications of AI use in your classroom. How will you ensure student privacy and data security?
5. Share what you've learned with a colleague. Discussing AI can help solidify your understanding and spark new ideas for implementation.

Remember, we're not aiming for "AI guru" status overnight. It's about taking those first steps towards integrating AI into your teaching practice in a way that enhances learning and lightens your workload.

Ready to move on to Part 2 and start implementing AI in the classroom? Let's go!

Part 2: Implementing AI in the Classroom

Chapter 4: Mastering the Art of AI Prompting

In our journey to use AI in education, we've reached a crucial skill: the art of effective prompting. Since Generative AI is trained on vast amounts of human language, your own language skills are key to getting the best results.

Just as we adjust our communication for different students, whether by simplifying concepts or increasing complexity, we need to adapt our prompts for AI to produce the most useful outputs.

The Five-Step Formula for Effective Prompting

Through my experience and research, I've developed a five-step formula that I find incredibly useful when crafting prompts for AI.

1. **Role**
   What role should the AI take on?

2. **AIM**
   What exactly do you want it to do?

3. **Audience**
   Who is the output for?

4. **Context**
   What background does the AI need to know?

5. **Constraints**
   What limits or directions should it follow?

Breaking Down the Five Steps for Effective AI Prompts

Now that we've introduced the five-step formula, let's explore each of these in more detail to understand how they can enhance your AI prompting approach.

Role: What perspective should the AI take on?
This step is about defining the role you want the AI to assume. The clearer you are with the role, the more focused and relevant the response will be. It helps shape the tone and depth of the output.

Example: *"Take on the role of a Year 9 history teacher."*
By specifying that the AI should "be" a teacher, you guide it to use more instructional language and focus on content suited to classroom settings.

Aim: What exactly do you need the AI to do?
Be specific about the task you're asking the AI to complete. The more clearly you define the aim, the better the AI's response will match your expectations.

Example: *"Create a 60-minute lesson on the causes of WWI."*
This ensures the AI knows the outcome you're seeking (in this case, a lesson plan) and provides a targeted response.

Audience: Who is the output for?
Knowing the audience is essential for adjusting the complexity and tone of the response. Whether you're tailoring it for younger students, EAL learners, or advanced students, stating this early ensures the AI responds appropriately.

Example: *"The lesson is for mixed-ability Year 9 students."*
This ensures the AI generates content that is accessible to all, including those who may need additional support.

Context: What background information is important?
Providing context helps the AI incorporate relevant background details. This step allows you to include specifics that ensure the response is well-suited to the environment you're working in.

Example: *"This is their first WWI lesson. They have limited knowledge of early 20th-century politics."*
With this context, the AI understands that the students may need foundational concepts before delving into more complex material.

Constraints: What limitations should the AI follow?
Set boundaries for the output, such as time limits, content restrictions, or specific elements to include or avoid. Constraints ensure the AI doesn't wander off topic or provide too much unnecessary information.

Example: *"Include three main activities, each 15 minutes. Avoid military jargon."*
These constraints keep the AI's response structured, focused, and appropriate for the classroom setting.

Practical Application: Using the Five-Step Formula

Let's put this formula into practice with a real-world teaching scenario:

Role: Experienced Year 9 English teacher
Aim: Create a lesson plan for introducing Shakespeare's "Romeo and Juliet"
Audience: Year 9 students with mixed reading abilities
Context: This is the students' first exposure to Shakespeare
Constraints: The lesson should be 40 minutes long and include at least one interactive activity

Complete prompt: *"As an experienced Year 9 English teacher, create a 60-minute lesson plan for introducing Shakespeare's 'Romeo and Juliet' to Year 9 students with mixed reading abilities. This is the students' first exposure to Shakespeare. The lesson should include at least one interactive activity."*

Common Pitfalls in AI Prompting

While effective prompting can unlock AI's potential, there are a few common mistakes to avoid:

Being Too Vague: A prompt like "Tell me about World War II" is too broad. The AI won't know what aspect you're interested in or at what level. You might get a response aimed at Year 13 students when you really need something suitable for Year 8.

Assuming Knowledge: Even though AI has access to a massive amount of information, it doesn't "know" your specific classroom context unless you tell it.

Neglecting the Audience: Forgetting to specify the intended audience can lead to content that's either too advanced or too simplistic.

Overcomplicating the Prompt: While details are important, too much information can overwhelm the AI and lead to less useful outputs.

Forgetting Ethical Considerations: Always remember the ethical implications of your prompts, especially when dealing with sensitive topics or student data.

Ethical Considerations in Prompting

As educators, we have a responsibility to ensure we're using AI ethically. Here are a few key points to keep in mind:

- **Privacy:** Avoid including real names or identifiable student data in your prompts. Instead, use generic placeholders like "Student A."
- **Bias Awareness:** AI models are trained on real-world data, which can include biases. Always review the output critically, especially when dealing with sensitive or controversial topics.

- **Accuracy:** AI can generate plausible-sounding but incorrect information. Double-check important facts before using AI-generated content in your classroom.
- **Personalising Outputs:** Use AI-generated content as a starting point. Adapt and personalise it based on your classroom's unique needs and learning objectives.

And don't worry about being "experts" in ethics – keeping these simple guidelines in mind is enough to make a positive impact when using AI in your teaching practice.

Something to Remember

Sometimes, conversations with an AI flow smoothly, and other times, they can feel a bit clunky.

It's a lot like talking to people—some interactions click, while others are awkward and you just want to move on (though with AI, at least starting over is a lot easier!).
The key is recognising that it's an ongoing process of trial and error and learning how to adjust when things don't work out as expected.

Chapter 5: Practical Applications in the Classroom

Now that we've covered how to craft effective prompts, let's roll up our sleeves and explore practical uses of Generative AI in day-to-day teaching.

I'll share examples from my own classroom and training workshops at my school, using the Five-Step Formula to guide each prompt.

Lesson Planning

Role: Experienced Year 9 History teacher
Aim: Create a 60-minute lesson outline on the causes of World War I
Audience: Year 9 students
Context: Students have some knowledge of 20th-century history but haven't covered WWI in detail
Constraints: Include three learning objectives, a 10-minute introduction, and two key activities

Complete prompt: *"As an experienced Year 9 History teacher, create a 60-minute lesson outline on the causes of World War I for Year 9 students. They have some knowledge of 20th-century history but haven't covered World War I. Include three learning objectives, a 10-minute introduction, and two main activities."*

Retrieval Practice Questions

Role: Secondary school Maths teacher
Aim: Generate three sets of retrieval practice questions on solving quadratic equations
Audience: Students at different ability levels
Context: The students have learned about quadratic equations but are at varying stages of understanding
Constraints: Ensure each set progressively increases in difficulty

Complete prompt: *"As a secondary Maths teacher, generate three sets of retrieval practice questions on solving quadratic equations for students at different ability levels. The students have previously learned about quadratic equations but are at varying stages of understanding. Each set should progressively increase in difficulty."*

Assessment

Role: Year 10 English teacher
Aim: Create 10 multiple-choice questions on Chapter 3 of To Kill a Mockingbird
Audience: Year 10 students
Context: Students have read Chapters 1 and 2, and the focus should be on comprehension and character analysis
Constraints: Questions should be a mix of recall, inference, and analysis

Complete prompt: *"As a Year 10 English teacher, create 10 multiple-choice questions on Chapter 3 of To Kill a Mockingbird. The students have already read Chapters 1 and 2, and the focus should be on comprehension and character analysis. The questions should be a mix of recall, inference, and analysis."*

Supporting Learners

Role: Science teacher for lower secondary
Aim: Simplify a paragraph on climate change
Audience: Year 7 student with a reading age of 9
Context: The student needs content that is accessible and easy to understand without losing key information
Constraints: Keep the language simple but ensure the core ideas remain intact

Complete prompt: *"As a Science teacher, simplify a paragraph on climate change for a Year 7 student with a reading age of 9. The content should remain accurate, but the language should be simplified for better understanding."*

Role: History teacher for Key Stage 2
Aim: Support a Year 5 student with ADHD in completing a project on the Romans
Audience: Year 5 student with a reading age of 8
Context: The student needs guidance on structuring a project on Roman life, focusing on making the task accessible, manageable, and engaging
Constraints: Break the project into small, structured steps, using visual aids, timers, and rewards to support focus and motivation. Tailor the project to meet the student's IEP targets, such as improving attention, following instructions, and staying organised.

Complete Prompt: *"As a History teacher, help a Year 5 student with ADHD and a reading age of 8 complete a project on Roman life. Break down the task into smaller, structured steps to support their focus and engagement. Incorporate SEND strategies such as visual aids (pictures of Roman soldiers and buildings), timers for task management, and regular breaks. Consider the student's IEP targets, including improving attention span, following multi-step instructions, and staying organised. Offer scaffolding, chunking, and clear instructions to help the student successfully complete the project."*

Administrative Tasks

Role: Head of English Department
Aim: Generate an agenda for a 30-minute meeting on improving GCSE English Literature results
Audience: English department staff
Context: The meeting will focus on strategies to boost student performance in English Literature exams
Constraints: Include time for discussion, review of recent results, and brainstorming new teaching approaches

Complete prompt: *"As the Head of English Department, generate a 30-minute meeting agenda for improving GCSE English Literature results. The meeting will focus on strategies to boost student performance and should include time for discussion, a review of recent results, and brainstorming new teaching approaches."*

Ask for Best Practices, But Stay Critical

When using AI, asking it to follow best practices can really enhance the output—especially when you're working with unconventional materials. For example, I often use AI to help plan meeting agendas by inputting the resources I have on hand, like post-its, A3 paper, and markers, and asking for brainstorming techniques.

However, while AI can provide great ideas, it's important to stay cautious. AI has been trained on a vast range of information, including outdated practices and educational myths (edumyths) like VAK learning styles. This means it might sometimes suggest methods that have been debunked.

That's why it's crucial to always review AI's suggestions critically, applying your own knowledge and expertise to make sure the ideas are current, evidence-based, and effective.

Using AI to Enhance Your Lesson Plans

When it comes to using AI in the classroom, starting with something familiar is a smart move. Planning a lesson is an ideal place to begin. You know your subject inside out, so asking AI to help you plan lets you compare its suggestions with your own ideas. Many AI platforms even toss in a sparkle emoji to add a bit of magic to the process—though, let's face it, as teachers we already add plenty of sparkle to our lessons.

From my experience it is a great starting point, but there are more powerful ways to use it.

But where AI really shines is in offering feedback on what you've already planned. You don't need AI to tell you how to teach; you already know what works for your students. But by using AI as an assistant, you gain an extra set of eyes on your lesson plan, enriched by a broad base of educational practices you might not have considered.

You can type up your outline or upload the resources you plan to use, then ask for feedback. AI can help check if your lesson meets the needs of all your students, including those with SEND or your most able learners. It can also scan your plan for any unintentional bias or point out where something might be unclear or could lead to confusion.
This use of AI doesn't replace your expertise, it enhances it. By offering an additional layer of insight, AI helps you create lessons that are not just good, but outstanding, pushing your plans from simple feedback to real feedforward.

Why not try using advanced voice mode tools to take this even further?

With these features, you can have a real conversation with AI, verbalising your lesson ideas and asking it to act as a critical friend. This back-and-forth can help you refine ideas, highlight any weak spots, and even spark new approaches; all without having to type a single word.

Counteracting Bias in AI Outputs

Before we dive in, it's important to recognise that AI models often reflect societal biases present in their training data. This is particularly evident in image generation prompts. For instance, if you ask an AI to generate images of "doctors", you might primarily see images of white men. This bias isn't from the AI itself, but from the data we humans have fed it, reflecting historical imbalances.

As educators, we're responsible for providing balanced, inclusive content. When using AI, it's crucial to be aware of these potential biases and actively work to counteract them. Here's how:

- **Ask for Diverse Perspectives:** Don't settle for the first response. Prompt the AI to consider multiple viewpoints. For example: "Now, provide an alternative perspective on this historical event from a different cultural standpoint."
- **Specify Inclusivity in Your Prompts:** Make inclusivity a clear requirement. Try: "Create a reading list for our Victorian Literature unit, ensuring representation of diverse authors including women, people of colour, and those from working-class backgrounds."
- **Check and Challenge Assumptions:** If you notice bias, ask the AI to reconsider. For instance: "Your previous response seemed to assume all students have internet access at home. Please revise the homework plan to include offline alternatives."

Example Prompt

Role: Key Stage 3 English Literature Coordinator
Aim: Develop a unit on 'Heroes and Villains in Literature'
Audience: Year 8 teachers and students
Context: Updating our curriculum to be more representative and culturally diverse

Constraints: Include texts from a variety of cultures and time periods, ensure a balance of male and female authors, and incorporate stories that challenge traditional hero/villain narratives.

Remember, AI is a tool, not an authority. Your critical thinking and commitment to inclusivity are key to creating truly representative and balanced educational content. Keep questioning, keep refining, and you'll be using AI to create a more inclusive learning environment for all your students.

Supercharging Your AI Outputs

Want AI-generated content that feels like it was made just for your school? Here's how to make it happen:

- **Give AI Some Examples:** Show AI what you like. If you want a lesson plan in your style, give it one you've already made. It's like training a new colleague.
- **Align with Your School's Style:** Mention your school's unique approach in your prompts. For example: "Create a lesson plan that incorporates our school's values of resilience, respect, and responsibility."
- **Be Specific About Your Needs:** The more detail you give, the better. Instead of asking for "a maths lesson", try "a Year 9 maths lesson on quadratic equations, incorporating our school's 'think-pair-share' strategy."

Here are two examples of this in action:

Role: Key Stage 2 History Coordinator
Aim: Develop a scheme of work for the Vikings topic
Audience: Year 5 teachers
Context: We're updating our curriculum to be more inclusive and inquiry-based
Constraints: Include opportunities for cross-curricular links, embed our school's 'Growth Mindset' approach, and suggest ways to involve our local community

Role: Year 8 Science Teacher
Aim: Create a lesson plan on the water cycle
Audience: Mixed ability Year 8 class
Context: This is part of the Earth Science unit in the Key Stage 3 curriculum
Constraints: Use the "I Do, We Do , You Do" approach, incorporate a hands-on experiment, and include formative assessment opportunities

By feeding AI your examples, school values, and specific needs, you're creating a personalised assistant that speaks your educational language. This isn't just about using AI, it's about moulding it to amplify your teaching.

In Case of Emergency

When you're staring at a blank AI chat, unsure where to even begin...that's when you pull out the Emergency Prompt.

It's the ultimate lifeline for those moments when you're completely stuck and have no idea where to start.
Here's the beauty of it: you can use AI to help you get started with AI. Sounds meta, right? But it works.

Just type in:

You are [X]. The task I want to complete is [Y]. What additional information or context do you need from me to assist with this task effectively?

It's like giving the AI a nudge, inviting it to ask you the right questions and help you lay out the steps.
Whether you're trying to plan a lesson, organise a project, or write up a report, this Emergency Prompt cuts through any "prompters block".

Now, fair warning—sometimes AI might start asking a lot of questions, some of which might feel unnecessary. That's fine! Just answer the ones that feel relevant to you and skip the rest. But remember, the more direction and details you can give, the better the AI's output will be.

It's the perfect kickstart when you're feeling lost, ensuring you and the AI are working in sync.

Chapter 6. Ideas on How to Use Generative AI in the Classroom

While AI is powerful tool that can support our teaching, figuring out how to integrate it meaningfully into lessons? That's where things get tricky.

The prompt in this chapter is designed to help with exactly that—it's a guide to help you explore creative ways to bring generative AI into your classroom.

Featured in *Forbes* for its innovative approach, this prompt helps you find practical ways to use AI in teaching while ensuring fairness, transparency, and privacy. It's all about showing you how to use AI effectively, without compromising on ethics.

The prompt offers ideas for using AI in lessons, often through what I call "AI by Proxy"—where you, the teacher, use AI while students observe.

Take an English lesson, for example: students could create descriptive prompts for images, which you then input into the AI for the class to review.

This gives everyone a chance to analyse the language, critique the generated image, and improve their prompts, all while building valuable AI and language skills.

Here's the prompt I developed:

"As an expert in AI-driven education with a specialisation in formulating prompts for Generative AI, you recognise the profound impact and responsibility of implementing AI in educational settings. Keeping in mind the ethical implications, ask me for the year group, subject, and learning objectives for my lesson.
You will then offer recommendations on integrating Generative AI prompts into my lessons to deepen understanding, ensuring transparency, fairness, and privacy.
Your focus will be on platforms like ChatGPT and text-to-image generators. When creating scenarios where generative AI assumes the role of a character or object, you will also provide example prompts. These prompts are designed not only for effective role embodiment but also to maintain respectful and unbiased interactions during the session.
You will encourage open discussions on the ethical boundaries and best practices when deploying these AI tools in the classroom."

This isn't just about throwing AI into your lessons and hoping for the best.

It's about using AI purpose-intentionally creating opportunities for deeper learning while staying conscious of its ethical implications.

Scan this QR code to access the prompt as a GPT called "ClassAI".

Chapter 7. The PAIR Framework for AI Integration

As we explore integrating AI into our classrooms, it's immensely helpful to have a structured approach.
I suggest the PAIR Framework, developed by researchers at King's College London. This framework offers a practical, step-by-step method for incorporating AI into our teaching practices responsibly and effectively.

In my experience, I've found that PAIR works best for individual implementation, taking a bottom-up approach. It's particularly valuable for addressing real-world scenarios we face daily as educators.

For those interested in broader implementation, don't worry - I've got that covered too. In Chapter 10, we'll explore a comprehensive roadmap for adopting AI across an entire school.

What is the PAIR Framework?

PAIR stands for Problem formulation, AI tool selection, Interaction, and Reflection.

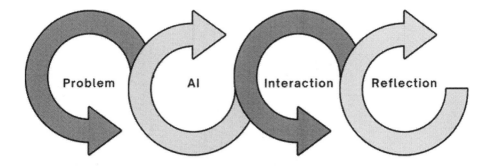

Exploring the PAIR Framework

Step 1. Problem Formulation

The first step is to clearly define the specific educational challenge or goal you want to address with AI. It's about identifying what you're trying to achieve before deciding which AI tool to use.

Example: You might notice students struggle with real-world problem-solving in maths.

Step 2. AI Tool Selection

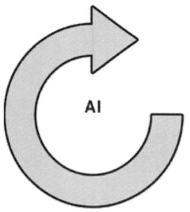

Once you've defined your problem, it's time to choose the right AI tool to solve it. This step involves researching various tools and evaluating their features (check out appendix 1).

Example: You might explore AI-powered tools that generate text to create real-world math problems.

Step 3. Interaction

This stage is all about using the AI tool in your teaching. You'll also want to monitor the tool's impact on learning outcomes.

Example: You might start by using the tool to generate weekly problem-solving challenges, watching how students engage with them.

Step 4. Reflection

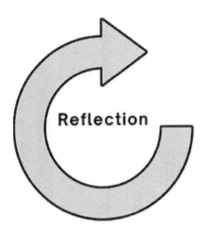

Finally, step back and evaluate how well the AI integration worked. Consider what went well, what didn't, and how the process can be improved for the next cycle.

Example: After a few weeks of using the AI tool, reflect on student progress. Did the tool help? If not, how can you tweak its use?

Applying the PAIR Framework

Now that we have explored the PAIR Framework, it is time to put it into action by working through and completing the four stages below:

Step 1. Problem Formulation

Define your educational challenge or goal:

Step 2. AI Tool Selection

What AI tool did you choose to address the problem:

Step 3. Interaction

Describe how you will implement the AI tool:

Step 4. Reflection

Evaluate how well the tool worked and what to adjust:

In the online version of *AI in Education: An Educator's Handbook*, you'll discover a ready-to-use template of the PAIR framework, crafted to support you in integrating AI seamlessly into your teaching. Just scan the QR code below:

Part 2 Recap

Well, we've certainly rolled up our sleeves in Part 2, haven't we? We've cracked the code on how to talk to AI (it's all about those prompts), and we've explored some real-world ways to bring AI into our lessons.

Key Takeaways:

1. Crafting AI prompts is just like having a conversation; it's about being clear and specific in what you're asking. The more you chat with AI, the more natural it becomes.
2. AI isn't just for planning; it can help with everything from assessments to supporting learners with different needs.
3. The PAIR Framework isn't just another acronym to memorise; it's a practical tool for bringing AI into your classroom responsibly.
4. Using AI doesn't mean losing the human touch. It's about freeing up time for more meaningful interactions with our students.
5. Ethical use of AI isn't an afterthought; it's embedded

Part 3: Navigating Challenges and Building Partnerships

Chapter 8: Addressing Challenges and Concerns

Let's face it: bringing AI into education isn't all smooth sailing. We're bound to hit some rough patches and face some tough questions along the way. But here's the thing - we can't just sweep these issues under the rug.

We need to tackle them head-on, with a good dose of common sense and ethics. So, let's dive into the most common concerns educators are grappling with and hash out some practical ways to tackle these challenges head on.

Ethical Concerns

Educators should have a basic understanding of the ethical considerations related to AI, but they don't need to be experts.

It's more important to collaborate with key staff, such as the IT team and those responsible for GDPR and safeguarding, to ensure AI tools are used responsibly and in line with school policies.

In this chapter, we're going to take a whirlwind tour of the main ethical areas you should have on your radar.

Privacy and Data Security

One of the big worries with AI is making sure our students' data stays under wraps. Here's how we can keep things secure while still making the most of what AI has to offer:

- **Stick to Approved Tools:** Use AI tools that have been approved by your school's SLT first, then the IT department. Got a new tool in mind? Run it by them first to make sure it meets school policy.

- **Anonymise Data:** When possible, avoid using actual student names or sensitive information. Use pseudonyms, initials, or student ID numbers to protect their identities.
- **Communicate with Students and Parents:** Explain to both students and parents how AI tools are being used and the privacy measures in place. If necessary, seek parental consent.
- **Check Privacy Policies:** Get to know the privacy policies of the AI tools you're planning to use. Pay attention to how data is stored, shared, and whether you have control over managing or deleting it.
- **Teach Digital Privacy:** Teach students about digital privacy. It's not just about addressing concerns - it's about empowering them to look after their own data in the digital world.

Fairness and Bias

AI tools can sometimes perpetuate biases based on the data they're trained on. Here's how we can aim to keep things fair:

- **Review AI Outputs Critically:** Always give AI-generated content a once-over. Keep an eye out for any stereotypes or biases in how it portrays different genders, jobs, or cultures.
- **Diversify Your Sources:** Use multiple tools and data sources to gather broader perspectives, especially in subjects where bias could influence understanding. Ideally, use AI web tools that search the web and/or provide references, like Perplexity or MS Copilot. A good "old-fashioned" web search to cross-check information is also encouraged for added accuracy.
- **Make Bias a Part of the Lesson:** Use AI's shortcomings as a teachable moment. Talk to your students about how bias creeps into AI systems and why it's crucial to question the information AI serves up.

Managing Parental Concerns

Bringing AI into the classroom could raise a few eyebrows among parents, especially when it comes to privacy, data security, and the role of tech in learning. Here's how we can get parents on board:

- **Transparent Communication:** Keep parents informed about how AI is used in your classroom. Lay out your goals, the tools you're using, and how you're keeping student data safe.
- **Seek Consent When Necessary:** If you are using AI tools with students aged 13 to 18, ensure you seek parental consent for platforms that require it (see appendix 1 for guidance on the listed AI tools).
- **Highlight the Benefits:** Focus on the ways AI can support learning, such as reducing teacher workload, and preparing students to work with AI tools in the future.

Student Misuse of AI

Another challenge educators are concerned about is students using AI tools inappropriately, such as relying too heavily on AI for assignments. However, recent studies, including data from Turnitin, show that the misuse of AI in assessments is not as widespread as initially feared. In fact, AI usage in cheating is minimal, suggesting that concerns over AI misuse are becoming a new "edumyth".

These are my recommendations:

- **Trust goes a long way:** At our school, we operate on a trust-based system. We don't routinely use plagiarism detection platforms unless an exam board requires it. This approach fosters a culture of responsibility and integrity among students.

- **Get to know your students early:** Start the year with exercises that really showcase each student's individual voice. Personal narratives, opinion pieces, or creative projects can give you a clear sense of their authentic style.
- **Teachable Moments:** If you do suspect AI misuse, your relationship with the student allows for open, constructive conversations. It's not about catching them out, try to find out why they used AI.
- **Encouraging Authentic Voice:** When students know you value their unique perspectives and writing styles, they're more likely to take pride in their own work. It's all about them feeling seen, heard, and valued.

AI's Environmental Footprint

While AI is an incredible tool for education, its environmental cost, particularly in text and image generation, shouldn't be overlooked. For instance, generating a single AI image uses as much energy as charging a smartphone, and producing a short AI-generated email can consume the equivalent of a bottle of water due to the cooling needs of data centres.

Ironically, AI could help combat the very problem it contributes to. Researchers are already using AI to model climate change, optimise renewable energy, and design carbon-capturing technologies. The hope is that, while today's models demand substantial resources, they may eventually aid in resolving the climate crisis they partly fuel.

Classroom Discussion Points:

- **Energy Use:** How much power is required for AI models?
- **Sustainability:** How can we use AI responsibly?
- **AI for Good:** Can AI help solve climate challenges it contributes to?

By posing these questions, educators can encourage students to critically assess technology's trade-offs while exploring AI's potential role in climate solutions. Discussing the hidden costs of digital tools, alongside their advantages, nurtures a well-rounded understanding of AI's place in the modern world.

Encouraging students to reflect on their own technology use can link personal habits to global sustainability efforts.
By weaving environmental ethics into AI education, students not only learn about AI but also develop the critical thinking needed for responsible innovation.
As we continue to explore AI's possibilities, it's worth pausing to consider the unseen costs. Every version we generate requires energy, every iteration leaves a footprint.

So before hitting "generate" again—stop and think, is another generation necessary?

What If the Internet Goes Down?

There is a fear we, and our students, are becoming too dependent on tech, especially AI. It's a worry I hear a lot, but you know what? I actually see this as a positive shift in our thinking.

Sure, AI makes my job easier and turbocharges my workflow. But here's the kicker - I can still function just fine without it.

This whole debate about relying too much on AI? It's actually a good thing!

It's making us think, discuss and refocus on skills that really matter - critical thinking, communication, problem-solving. Let's be honest, we should've been giving these more airtime all along. These aren't just nice-to-haves. The World Economic Forum has been shouting from the rooftops for years that these skills are essential. It's high time we gave them the spotlight they deserve.

Instead of fretting about overusing AI, let's flip the script. This is our chance to focus on skills that will allow students to become adaptable, resourceful and resilient.

So, the next time someone asks, "But what if the internet goes down?", here's what you tell them: "Then we'll have a classroom full of students who can think critically, communicate effectively, and problem-solve like pros - with or without AI by their side."

Working with Hesitant Teachers

Introducing AI into education can ruffle some feathers, especially among teachers who might feel overwhelmed by these new tools or worry that AI might put them out of a job.

The key here is to focus on practical, hands-on experiences that show educators how AI can make their daily work easier and more effective:

- **Focus on the here and now:** Ask teachers to bring a task they're currently working on, like planning a lesson or grading assignments. During the hands-on sessions, walk them through using AI tools to help with that task. For example, show them how ChatGPT can whip up differentiated activities in no time.
- **Start small, think big:** Begin with one or two simple AI tools that are easy to use (Chapter 3 and Appendix 1 will help with this). Encourage teachers to focus on a single task, like generating retrieval practice questions or real-world problems for students to solve. These small wins will show them how AI can lighten their workload, making them more open to exploring AI further.
- **Create a buddy system:** Encourage teachers who've successfully integrated AI into their teaching to share their experiences with colleagues. Peer learning can inspire hesitant teachers to give AI a shot themselves.

- **Keep the learning going:** As AI tools keep evolving, it's important to offer regular workshops or drop-in sessions where teachers can experiment with new tools and features, keeping them up to date and comfortable with AI.

This One is More Legal than Ethical

You might have heard whispers about the EU AI Act, and how it has classified some AI systems based on risk.
Risk Categories for AI Systems:

- **Unacceptable Risk:** AI systems that manipulate behaviour, exploit vulnerable students, or use social scoring are strictly prohibited.
- **High Risk:** AI tools that significantly influence academic performance, such as automated grading or admission systems, require strict scrutiny and transparency.
- **Limited Risk:** Systems like language translation tools and AI-based content creation tools pose a lower risk but still need to be monitored.
- **Minimal Risk:** AI systems like spam filters or AI-enhanced educational games fall under minimal risk but still must comply with transparency rules.

Good news! Most of the AI tools and systems we're likely to use in schools fall under the minimal or limited risk categories.

If you're using tools like ChatGPT to create lesson content, remember to double-check the outputs. We've touched on this throughout the guide, but it bears repeating

Now, for any student-facing AI chatbots or 'Edubots'. They're officially classified as Limited Risk, but some schools have decided to rate them higher internally. It all depends on how and when students are interacting with them. Remember, these are guidelines. You can always err on the side of caution based on your school community's needs.

AI Literacy is Going Legal

Another big takeaway from the EU AI Act, is that starting February 5, 2025, companies in the EU need to provide AI literacy training if their employees are using AI. And guess what? Schools are no exception!

The EU AI Act might seem complex beast, but it's all about using AI responsibly and ethically in our schools.

I hosted a webinar breaking down the EU AI Act, which you can access using the QR code below.

Chapter 9. Engaging with EdTech and AI Companies

As AI tools continue to flood the education space, it's more important than ever for educators to navigate the world of EdTech and AI with confidence.

In this chapter, you'll find practical strategies for assessing AI tools, the key questions to ask, and guidance on making smart, informed choices when bringing AI into your school.
Remember, it's crucial to have a clear goal in mind before diving into any conversation with an EdTech company.

Key Criteria for Evaluating EdTech Tools

1. **Clear Educational Goals:** Make sure the tool supports your teaching objectives, whether they are short-term or long-term.
2. **Privacy and Data Security:** Ensure student data is handled securely and in compliance with relevant laws.
3. **Support and Training:** The company should offer effective training and continuous support to help you implement the tool.
4. **Flexibility and Customisation:** The tool should be adaptable to different teaching styles, learning levels, and integrate with existing systems.
5. **Ethical Use and Bias Prevention:** The AI should minimise bias, and the company should be transparent about how the tool was developed.
6. **Company Commitment to Education:** Look for vendors that understand education and are willing to collaborate with teachers and schools.
7. **Pricing and Scalability:** The tool should be affordable, with transparent pricing and the ability to scale if you expand its use.

8. **Trial and Pilot Options:** Before fully committing, see if the company offers a trial or pilot programme to test the tool in a real classroom setting.

Key Criteria for Evaluating EdTech Tools

When you're evaluating EdTech companies, use this table to track your questions and ensure you cover all key aspects of each tool. This format helps you keep everything organised and makes it easy to tick off questions during your discussion.

Question	Tick
Privacy and Data Security	
What student data does your tool collect, and how is it stored?	
Is student data anonymised, and how is it secured?	
Can you provide documentation proving compliance with privacy laws such as GDPR or COPPA?	
Who has access to the student data, and how long is it stored?	
How do you manage data breaches, and what protocols are in place?	
Support and Training	
What types of training do you offer for staff—online, in-person, or both?	
Is training included in the price, or does it come at an additional cost?	
Do you offer ongoing support after purchase? If so, what does that include?	
How quickly do you respond to support queries or technical issues?	
Will there be a dedicated point of contact for our school?	
What are your help desk hours and methods of contact (e.g., phone, email, chat)?	
Flexibility and Customisation	

Can this tool be customised to meet the specific needs of different age groups, subjects, or learning levels?	
Does your tool integrate with existing systems like our LMS (e.g., Google Classroom, Microsoft Teams)?	
Can the tool be adapted based on feedback from teachers and students?	
Are there options for customisation specific to our curriculum needs, and how flexible is this process?	
Ethical Use and Bias Prevention	
What steps have you taken to minimise bias in the AI's outputs?	
How was your AI trained, and what datasets were used in the process?	
How do you handle bias if it's found in the tool, and what steps are taken to fix it?	
What safeguards are in place to ensure the AI is fair and inclusive for all students?	
Company Commitment to Education	
Can you share case studies or examples of how your tool has been successfully used in other schools?	
How do you engage with educators to improve your product?	
Are you involved in educational research or pilot programmes with schools?	
Pricing and Scalability	
What is your pricing structure? Is it per student, class, or school?	
Are there any additional fees for support, updates, or new features?	
Can this tool be scaled for use in more classes or across multiple departments?	
How do you handle pricing if we expand to a school-wide or multi-school/campus rollout?	
Trial and Pilot Options	
Do you offer a pilot programme or trial period so we can test the tool in a real classroom setting?	

What features are included in the trial, and how long does it last?	
Will you be able to adjust the tool based on feedback from our pilot programme?	
What kind of support do you offer during the pilot period to ensure a smooth trial?	

Part 3 Recap

Part 3 got into the nitty-gritty of implementing AI in education. Here, we've faced head-on the big questions and concerns that come with this technological shift. Ethical considerations, worries about student misuse, and even the environmental impact of AI all came under the microscope. This section also explored strategies for effective collaboration with EdTech and AI companies, ensuring we're equipped to choose the right tools for our classrooms.

Key Takeaways:

1. Ethical use of AI in education is about awareness and making informed decisions, not becoming an ethics expert overnight.
2. Concerns about student misuse of AI aren't as dire as we first thought - it's more about teaching responsible use.
3. The environmental impact of AI is a great topic for classroom discussions, linking technology use to wider global issues.
4. Engaging with EdTech and AI companies is all about asking the right questions and knowing what to look for in a tool.
5. Building partnerships with AI companies can lead to better, more education-focused tools.
6. From February 2025, AI literacy training will be a legal requirement in Europe, emphasizing the growing importance of AI education and beyond.

Next Steps:

1. Review your school's data protection policies. How do they apply to AI tools you're considering?
2. Have a frank discussion with your students about responsible AI use. What guidelines can you create together?
3. Use the checklist from Chapter 9 next time you're evaluating an AI or EdTech tool for your classroom.
4. Start a conversation with colleagues about creating an AI policy for your school. What should it include?

Remember, navigating the challenges of AI in education isn't about having all the answers right away. It's about asking good questions, staying informed, and always keeping our students' best interests at heart.

Ready to put all this together into an action plan? Let's move on to Part 4 and create your AI roadmap!

Part 4: Your AI Roadmap

Chapter 10. Your School's AI Roadmap

IImplementing AI across a whole school might seem like a big task, but with the right roadmap, it can be an

achievable and rewarding journey.
You might remember the **PAIR** Framework from Chapter 7, it's brilliant for individual classrooms and tasks. But when we're talking about rolling out AI on a school-wide scale, we need something bigger.

That's where the **Look**, **Book**, and **Cook** approach comes in.

Now, you might be wondering about the name. Well, being from Stoke-on-Trent, I've often been teased for saying "Luke," "Buke," and "Cuke" instead of "Look," "Book," and "Cook" when I'm outside the area.

But you know what? I've decided to take those words back and turn them into something that works for me. So, Look, Book, and Cook isn't just a nod to my accent…it's a framework for getting things done.

Look: Where You Are and Where You're Going

Adopting AI in education is an exciting step, but it's important not to rush into it. The temptation might be to dive straight into using the latest tools, but taking a moment to assess where your school stands can make all the difference. The foundation of any successful strategy lies in understanding both the current landscape and your goals for the future. Without this clear vision, any effort might end up being more about reacting to trends than creating meaningful change.

This is the moment to slow down, reflect, and ensure your plans are solid. By taking stock of your strengths, identifying gaps, and thinking about long-term objectives, you'll set yourself up for success. Think of this stage as the groundwork for building a sustainable and impactful AI strategy. It's a process that can help you be confident about the decisions you'll make moving forward.

Who Are Your Digital Champions?

Every school has those tech-savvy staff members who are naturally inclined to explore new digital tools. These people are your digital champions. They are the ones who can lead the way in adopting AI, experimenting with new tools, and supporting their colleagues along the journey. Equally important, however, are the staff who might need a little extra guidance. Both groups matter.

Understanding the range of skills within your team helps to tailor professional development in a way that is meaningful for everyone. You don't want to overwhelm anyone, but you do want to empower your team to feel confident in using AI tools effectively. I highly recommend assigning a member of your senior leadership team to oversee your AI initiative. Having someone in this role can ensure that AI is prioritised at a strategic level, not just seen as a passing experiment.

Is Your Tech Up to the Task?

Before getting carried away with the possibilities of AI, take a hard look at your school's infrastructure. Are your current devices, software, and internet capacity able to support AI tools? Do you have any filters or restrictions in place that could block access to the resources you need? Often, unblocking AI-powered tools is just the first step—there are usually other sub-parts, APIs, or connections that need to be unfiltered as well. A failure to do this could lead to frustrating roadblocks, especially during class time, when teachers and students are relying on the tools to work.

This is a key moment to ensure your technology is in line with your ambitions. It's no use planning for innovative AI tools if your infrastructure can't handle them. Make sure to test everything before fully committing, so you can avoid interruptions that may turn students off and make teachers hesitant to try again.

What's Already Working Well?

While it's easy to get swept up in the excitement of adopting new technology, it's important to recognise what your school is already doing well. Are there digital tools and systems that are currently thriving in your classrooms? Building on these successes can often be the most efficient and least disruptive way to introduce AI.

If certain AI tools or digital platforms have already been well-received in specific departments or with particular student groups, consider how you can expand their use school-wide. This approach helps maintain continuity and allows you to build on your current momentum. It also shows your staff and students that the transition to AI is part of an ongoing journey, not a sudden shift.

How Can We Get Everyone on Board?

The success of AI adoption doesn't just depend on the tools you choose or the technology you have in place, it's also about the people who will use it. Engaging teachers, students, parents, and administrators from the very beginning is vital. These are the people who will be most affected by AI, so their insights and perspectives should be central to your planning.

You might find that some are enthusiastic early adopters, while others might be more hesitant. Both perspectives are valuable. Encouraging open conversations about the potential benefits and challenges of AI will make the adoption process feel inclusive rather than imposed. This engagement fosters a culture of collaboration, where everyone feels like they are part of the journey, not just along for the ride.

Where Do You Want to Be in 5–10 Years?

It's easy to get caught up in the here and now, but when it comes to AI adoption, thinking long-term is essential. AI is evolving rapidly, and it has the potential to transform education in ways we are only just beginning to imagine. So where do you want your school to be in five or ten years? What role will AI play in that vision?

Thinking ahead helps ensure that your AI strategy isn't just about meeting immediate needs, but about preparing your school to stay ahead in an ever-changing educational landscape. Consider how AI might shape not only teaching and learning but also administration, communication, and student support. Setting a clear long-term vision will guide your short-term decisions, making sure they align with your broader goals.

Moving Forward

The Look phase of AI adoption is all about preparation. Before jumping into specific tools or strategies, you need to understand where you are, what you already have, and where you want to go. By identifying your digital champions, evaluating your infrastructure, recognising your existing strengths, and bringing your whole community on board, you'll lay a solid foundation for success. Most importantly, by setting a long-term vision, you'll ensure that your AI adoption isn't just a short-term fix, but a transformative journey that benefits your school for years to come.

Taking this time to look deeply at your current situation might feel like an extra step, but it's a critical one. The better you understand your starting point, the better equipped you'll be to navigate the road ahead.

Book: Your AI Playbook

With a solid understanding of where you stand and where you want to head, it's time to design the roadmap for your AI journey. This phase involves setting clear goals and outlining the steps to achieve them. A well-structured playbook not only helps guide your team but also ensures everyone is aligned with your school's long-term vision for AI integration.

Let's break down how to build this AI playbook, incorporating the crucial elements of goal-setting, responsible use, team readiness, and a robust AI policy to support your strategy.

Define What Success Looks Like

First, define what success means for your school when it comes to AI. What are your key objectives? Whether you're aiming to improve student outcomes, streamline administrative tasks, or enhance teaching practices, clear goals are essential.

Once your goals are set, break them into actionable steps. Alongside each step, identify potential evidence that will show progress—this might include feedback from staff, student engagement data, or documented improvements in processes. Make sure everyone agrees on how evidence will be collected and tracked to ensure consistency.

Use AI Responsibly

As you incorporate AI into your school, one of the most important aspects is ensuring that it's used ethically and responsibly. AI presents incredible opportunities, but it also raises critical concerns around data privacy, security, and fairness. Now is the time to create a policy that addresses these concerns head-on.

Imagine a student walks into your classroom wearing AI-enhanced wearables like Meta Ray-Bans, silently recording or using AI in real time. While this may sound futuristic, it's closer than we think. Schools need to be prepared for these kinds of scenarios, not just by reacting but by establishing clear guidelines and policies beforehand.

Developing a clear policy ensures that both staff and students understand the ethical and privacy implications of using AI. Your policy should cover everything from responsible data use to safeguarding student privacy and offer clear guidance on how AI should be integrated into daily practices. A robust policy provides structure and protects against misunderstandings or accidental misuse.

Equip Your Team for Success

Your AI journey won't succeed without the support and skills of your team. It's essential to invest in training and development to help staff feel confident using AI tools effectively. Offer collaborative learning sessions where staff can experiment with new tools and share best practices. Consider establishing a long-term professional development plan that allows staff to continually refine their skills as AI evolves.

Building AI competence across your team ensures smoother integration and increases the likelihood of long-term success. Encourage experimentation, creativity, and collaboration, so that your team feels empowered to make the most of AI tools.

Balance Quick Successes with Big Dreams

While it's vital to keep your long-term vision in sight, don't underestimate the power of quick wins. Small successes along the way can build momentum and boost morale, helping your team stay motivated throughout the journey. Whether it's enhancing a lesson plan or automating a simple administrative task, these early victories are worth celebrating.

At the same time, be sure that these smaller wins align with your broader strategy. Keep an eye on your big picture goals and ensure that the short-term gains contribute to your long-term vision for AI adoption in your school.

Create a Clear AI Policy

A strong AI strategy needs to be underpinned by a well-thought-out policy. Without a clear AI policy, schools risk chaotic or inconsistent implementation. An AI policy acts as the glue that holds everything together, ensuring that your school's culture, strategy, and ethical considerations all align.

Why Policy Matters

If culture drives excitement and strategy provides direction, policy is the framework that ensures everything runs smoothly. Without it, schools may find themselves unprepared for the complexities AI brings—whether that's around data protection, ethical use, or managing AI-enhanced devices that students may bring to school.

For example, a recent lawsuit in Massachusetts highlighted the importance of clear AI policies. A student accused of using AI to cheat on a history paper sparked a legal battle because the school lacked a clear policy on AI use. The school was focused on policing AI rather than guiding its responsible use, resulting in confusion and conflict.

Key Elements of an AI Policy

When crafting an AI policy for your school, keep these key questions in mind:

- **Ethical Use and Oversight:** How will your school ensure that AI is used ethically? Who will be responsible for overseeing AI implementation, and will there be a designated senior leader involved?
- **Data Privacy and Protection:** Which AI platforms are being considered, and are they GDPR compliant? How will staff be trained on responsible data sharing to ensure compliance with legal standards?

- **Teacher and Student Use Guidelines:** What guidance will help teachers confidently integrate AI into their lessons? How will appropriate AI use for students be defined to prevent misuse or over-reliance on technology?

Your AI policy should be flexible enough to adapt as the technology evolves but strong enough to set clear boundaries and expectations for everyone involved. By doing so, you not only protect your school but also foster an environment where AI can be used to its full potential.

Bringing It All Together: Culture, Strategy, and Policy

Think of AI integration as a three-legged stool: culture encourages innovation, strategy provides direction, and policy keeps everything grounded. Without all three working in harmony, the stool wobbles. Schools must ensure that their culture fosters experimentation with AI, their strategy provides a clear roadmap, and their policy offers the stability needed to keep everything on track.

Here's how these three elements can come together in a staff statement:

"We encourage staff to use Generative AI to assist with lesson planning, resource development, assessment creation, and administrative tasks. To help you, we've curated a list of AI tools that align with our school's values and standards. When using these tools, prioritise what genuinely enhances your practice. While AI can be a great assistant, your expertise remains key, always review AI-generated content before bringing it into the classroom. It's also essential to protect privacy and confidentiality: avoid sharing personal data or student information (such as names) with AI tools, and never upload confidential school documents to these platforms. All AI use must comply with our data protection and ethical guidelines. Have an idea for a new AI tool? Check with [insert school contact person]. We'd love your input on our AI approach too, consider joining our school's AI working party to share your ideas and experiences."

This statement reflects how cultural values, strategy, and policy all work together, ensuring that AI use is thoughtful, innovative, and responsible.

Moving Forward

The Book phase is all about creating a comprehensive, actionable plan that aligns with your school's goals and values. By setting clear objectives, developing responsible AI policies, equipping your team, and balancing short-term wins with long-term vision, you'll be well on your way to successful AI integration.

Remember, your AI playbook isn't just a one-time guide—it's a living document that will evolve as technology advances. Keep refining your approach, adapting to new developments, and engaging your team in the process. With a strong plan and a solid policy in place, your school will be well-positioned to harness AI's potential.

Cook: Implement, Evaluate, and Refine

Now that you've built your AI playbook, it's time to move from planning to action. The implementation phase is where your ideas are put into practice, but this isn't just a one-time effort. Effective implementation is an ongoing process that requires testing, gathering feedback, and making continuous adjustments. The key to success here is flexibility, responsiveness, and ensuring your initiative meets the needs of your school community.

Let's explore how you can roll out your AI plan with best practices for getting feedback, refining your approach, and staying ahead of the curve as technology evolves.

Start Small, Think Big

When rolling out an initiative like AI, starting small allows you to control and monitor the introduction of new tools. One best practice is to begin by piloting AI in select classes or departments. This initial rollout provides a manageable environment for testing and evaluating impact. By choosing a smaller group to trial these tools, you can gather useful data, observe outcomes, and make necessary adjustments before scaling up across the school.

This phased approach is often referred to as a "pilot programme." It allows you to learn quickly and refine your methods without overwhelming your entire staff or student body. Additionally, starting with a pilot group helps generate early success stories that you can use to build momentum and get broader buy-in from other departments.

Listening and Learning: Gathering Feedback

One of the most critical best practices for rolling out any new initiative is to establish a strong feedback loop. Listening to your team's insights will provide you with the real-world data needed to evaluate what's working and what isn't. Continuous feedback allows you to make real-time adjustments, ensuring that the AI tools you've implemented are meeting the needs of both staff and students.

Here are a few strategies for effective feedback collection:

- **Regular Check-ins:** Schedule routine meetings with the pilot team or department to discuss their experiences with AI. Ask for honest feedback about what's going well and where challenges are arising. These meetings provide a space for teachers to express their thoughts and for leadership to offer support or solutions.
- **Surveys:** Anonymous surveys can provide valuable insight, especially if staff feel hesitant to voice concerns in group settings. Design the survey to ask about specific AI tools, their ease of use, and their perceived impact on teaching and learning.
- **Student Feedback:** Don't forget to involve students in the feedback process. After all, they are the ultimate beneficiaries of AI in the classroom. Consider holding informal focus groups or issuing surveys to hear their thoughts on how AI is enhancing their learning experience.
- **Observation and Data Collection:** Alongside verbal feedback, monitor tangible outcomes. Are students more engaged? Are administrative tasks becoming more streamlined? Use measurable indicators like student engagement scores or time saved on administrative work to assess AI's impact.

Feedback is most effective when acted upon, so use this information to make adjustments as you go. A continuous cycle of listening and refining is essential for ensuring that AI tools are genuinely useful, not just new tech for the sake of it.

One Step at a Time: Gradual Rollout

Once you've gathered feedback from your pilot programme, the next step is to gradually scale up the initiative. One best practice here is to avoid rolling out too many AI tools at once. A staggered approach to implementation ensures that staff have the time and support they need to adapt to new technologies. Moving at a manageable pace also allows for thorough evaluation of each step before expanding further.

This phased rollout can follow a timeline, such as introducing AI tools to one department per term, or a gradual adoption within each department, starting with simpler applications before moving to more complex tools.

Ensure that ongoing professional development and training sessions are provided throughout the rollout. Staff need to feel confident and capable in using AI tools, and this confidence will grow as they become more familiar with the technology in stages.

Stay Ahead of the Curve: Continuous Learning

Best practices in education technology remind us that the landscape is always changing, and AI is no exception. AI is evolving rapidly, so it's important to foster a culture of continuous learning in your school. Encourage your staff to stay curious and to regularly explore new AI advancements and how they might fit into their teaching practices.

Consider these strategies for building a culture of continuous learning:

- **Professional Development:** Offer regular workshops, courses, or seminars focused on new developments in AI. Keep these learning opportunities hands-on and relevant to your school's needs so that staff can immediately see how AI can enhance their work.
- **Internal Learning Communities:** Create a space for teachers and administrators to share experiences and best practices around AI. A collaborative learning environment, such as a professional learning community (PLC), can be a great way for staff to support one another, troubleshoot problems, and exchange tips on effective AI use.
- **Dedicated AI Leadership:** Appoint or create a small AI leadership team who are responsible for staying informed on the latest trends and advancements. This team can regularly update the wider staff on new tools, offer guidance, and ensure the school remains at the cutting edge of AI in education.

Developing a Sustainable AI Culture

Creating a sustainable AI culture requires more than just adopting tools, it is about fostering an environment where experimentation, feedback, and continuous improvement are encouraged. When implementing AI, focus on how these tools align with your school's values and teaching goals. AI should not be a distraction but an enhancement that makes learning more engaging and teaching more efficient.

One best practice is to ensure that AI is integrated thoughtfully, solving real challenges rather than being adopted simply because it's available. Whether AI is used for streamlining administrative tasks, improving lesson planning, or enhancing student learning, it should be purposeful and aligned with your school's broader strategy.

Evaluating Your Progress

Evaluation is a crucial component of the implementation phase. You need to know if AI is truly delivering the results you envisioned. Here are some ways to ensure effective evaluation:
- **Data-Driven Insights:** Use both qualitative and quantitative measures to assess the impact of AI. For example, compare student engagement or performance before and after the introduction of AI tools. Similarly, track the time saved on administrative tasks or the level of staff satisfaction with the tools.
- **Iterative Evaluation:** Don't wait until the end of the school year to assess progress. Conduct regular check-ins at various stages of the implementation process to keep your approach flexible and responsive to feedback.
- **Success Stories:** Celebrate and share success stories within your school community. Highlight teachers or departments that are effectively using AI to inspire others and build excitement around the initiative.

Horizon Scanning: Keeping an Eye on the Future

As you implement and refine your AI strategy, it's important to stay aware of emerging trends and developments. Technology moves fast, and keeping up with the latest advancements ensures your school doesn't fall behind. Horizon scanning is about anticipating new tools, trends, and potential challenges that could shape the future of education.

Having someone on your team focused on this is essential. They need the time and capacity to regularly monitor these changes and keep leadership informed. This person should not only stay updated on the latest in AI but also consider how these innovations align with your school's goals.

While I enjoy following AI advancements, it can sometimes be overwhelming. This is where "many hands make light work." By having a team to share the responsibility and discuss new ideas, the task becomes more manageable. Together, they can stay on top of trends and, most importantly, make sure the school leadership receives timely updates to act on.

As I've said before, it's crucial that someone from the Senior Leadership Team (SLT) is either involved directly or fully onboard with this process.

By setting up a process for horizon scanning, your school will always be ready for what's coming next. It's not just about reacting to changes but about being proactive and fully prepared to seize new opportunities as they arise.

Moving Forward

The Cook phase is about more than just putting your AI plan into action. It's about learning, refining, and growing as you implement. Starting small, gathering feedback, and making adjustments at each stage ensures that your approach is sustainable and impactful. By moving one step at a time and maintaining open communication, you create a learning environment where AI can thrive.

Best practices such as piloting, continuous feedback, and phased rollouts ensure that your AI integration will be both thoughtful and effective. Stay adaptable, encourage continuous learning, and remember that AI implementation is a journey—one that, when done right, will transform your school for the better.

Let's Get Practical

Now it is time to turn these ideas into action. Over the next few pages, you will find three templates, one for each stage: Look, Book, and Cook.

I recommend accessing the free online version of this handbook using the QR code below to print these pages.

These templates will help you and your team organise your thoughts, set clear goals, and track your progress throughout the process. For more space to brainstorm, plan, and gather feedback, consider printing them on A3 or larger.

Let these templates guide you as you refine and adapt your AI approach.

LOOK: WHERE YOU ARE AND WHERE YOU'RE GOING

Goal: Assess your current situation, focusing on technology, skills, and tools.

Where do you want to be in 5-10 years?

Who Are Your Digital Champions?

Who Will Need Extra Support

What training can you offer, and who will lead it?

What tech updates or adjustments need to happen to ensure smooth adoption of AI platforms?

BOOK: WRITE YOUR AI PLAYBOOK

Now it's time for setting clear goals and defining the steps needed to achieve success with AI

What does success look like?	How will you measure it?

Your top 3 measurable goals for AI adoption	What are your quick wins?

Key Areas for an AI Policy
Discuss the refine your school's approach to these key areas:

Who Will Use the AI Tools?	Compliance with Regulations
Academic Integrity	**Data Privacy and Protection**
Transparency and Consent	**Ethical Use**

COOK: IMPLEMENT, EVALUATE, AND REFINE

This section will help you take the AI plan you've developed and put it into action, while focusing on continuous improvement.

Where can you start small?

Class or Department

AI Tools

Short-term goals

Timeline for introduction

(A) ─────────────────── (B)

How will you gather feedback?

What can you adjust or improve after the initial rollout?

What resources or networks will keep you updated on AI?

How will you share new AI insights with your team?

Chapter 11. Embracing the Future of Education

As we reach the end of our journey exploring AI in education, let's take a moment to reflect on what we've learned and look ahead to the exciting future we're building together.

Recap of Key Insights

Throughout this book, we've covered a lot of ground. Here are some of the key insights we've explored:

1. **AI as a Tool, Not a Replacement:** We've seen that AI is not here to replace teachers, but to enhance our capabilities. From generating learning materials to streamlining administrative tasks, AI allows us to focus more on what truly matters - inspiring and guiding our students.
2. **The Importance of Ethical Implementation:** We've discussed the crucial need for ethical considerations in AI use, including data privacy, fairness, and maintaining academic integrity. As educators, we have a responsibility to use AI in ways that protect and benefit our students.
3. **Practical Applications in the Classroom:** We've explored numerous ways to integrate AI into our teaching practice, from lesson planning and resource creation to assessment and feedback. These practical applications demonstrate the tangible benefits AI can bring to our daily work.
4. **The Need for Continuous Learning:** The field of AI is rapidly evolving, and we've emphasised the importance of ongoing professional development. Staying informed about AI advancements helps us make the most of these tools and prepare our students for an AI-driven future.

5. **Overcoming Challenges:** We've addressed common challenges in AI implementation, from technical barriers to pedagogical concerns. By anticipating these challenges, we can proactively develop strategies to overcome them.
6. **Strategic Implementation:** We've outlined a step-by-step approach to developing an AI implementation roadmap, emphasising the importance of careful planning, stakeholder engagement, and change management.

Part 4 Recap

You've reached the finish line of this AI in Education handbook. In this final part, you've tied everything together, crafting a practical roadmap for bringing AI into your entire school.

You're no longer just thinking about AI in isolated classrooms. Now, you've got the tools to implement a school-wide plan. This isn't about following trends; it's about leading the charge in educational innovation.

Take a moment to appreciate how far you've come. You started this journey perhaps feeling uncertain about AI, and now you're equipped to guide your whole school. That's no small feat - you should be proud of yourself!

Key Takeaways:

1. Successful AI implementation starts with understanding your school's current position and future goals.
2. The Look, Book, and Cook approach offers a systematic way to plan, implement, and refine your AI strategy.
3. Identifying and nurturing 'AI champions' within your staff can accelerate adoption and provide peer support.
4. Setting clear, measurable objectives is crucial for tracking the impact of AI on teaching and learning.
5. Balancing quick wins with long-term vision helps maintain momentum and stakeholder buy-in.

Next Steps:

1. Use the 'Look' template to assess your school's current AI readiness and identify areas for improvement.
2. Draft your school's AI vision using the 'Book' template, ensuring it aligns with your overall educational goals.
3. Implement a small-scale AI project using the 'Cook' template, focusing on gathering feedback and measuring impact.
4. Organise a workshop with key staff members to discuss and refine your school's AI implementation roadmap.
5. Schedule regular check-ins to review progress, address challenges, and update your AI strategy as needed.

Encouragement for Your AI Journey

As you embark on this AI journey, remember it's not about reaching a final destination, but about continuous learning and growth. Every step forward, no matter how small, is a triumph. Start with a single AI tool and let your natural curiosity guide you as you explore its potential. Implement AI across your school gradually. Start small, celebrate your successes, and don't be afraid to adjust your approach.

Regularly reflect on how AI is shaping your teaching and your students' learning, always keeping their needs at the heart of your efforts.

As you gain confidence and expertise, consider becoming an advocate for responsible AI use in education. Your efforts today will ripple out, positively impacting countless students and fellow educators.

You're not just keeping up with the future of education - you're actively shaping it. Every day, you're part of this exciting future.

So, take that first step with confidence. **What will your first move be?**

Appendix 1. Useful AI Tools

Over the next few pages, I've gathered a variety of AI platforms for you to explore. Many of these are rated 18+, though some can be used with students as young as 13 (with parental permission). Student facing chatbot platforms, like Mindjoy, are 18+ for teacher setup but the bots can be shared with students via links or logins.

You'll notice some rows highlighted – these are the tools I currently use in my workflow. But your flow will be different from mine, so feel free to pick, choose, and experiment with what works best for you!

Always check with your Senior Leadership Team (SLT) and IT department to ensure these tools are safe and accessible in your school.

AI Tool	Description	Pricing	Age
Adobe Firefly	AI for creating images and graphics, part of Adobe's creative suite.	Free	13+ (Parental permission required)
Beautiful.ai	AI-powered tool for creating professional presentations with design suggestions.	Paid	18+
Bing Image Creator	Generates images from text prompts, integrated with Microsoft Bing.	Free	13+ (Parental permission required)
Brisk	AI teaching assistant that helps with grading, lesson planning, and feedback.	Free	13+ (Parental permission required)

Canva for Education (Magic Tools)	A graphic design tool offering free premium features for educators and students. Magic tools are available for teachers to generate text, while students can only generate images, not text.	Free	13+ (Parental permission required)
Character AI	AI allowing users to interact with custom virtual characters.	Free	13+ (Parental permission required)
ChatGPT (OpenAI)	Conversational AI for generating text.	Free & Paid	13+ (Parental permission required)
Claude (Anthropic)	Conversational AI for generating text.	Free & Paid	18+
Copilot (Microsoft)	AI assistant integrated into Microsoft 365 for writing, coding, and more.	Paid	18+
Curipod	AI-powered tool for creating interactive lessons and presentations for the classroom.	Free & Paid	13+ (Parental permission required)
DALL·E 2 (OpenAI)	AI-powered image generation tool from OpenAI. Built into ChatGPT.	Free & Paid	13+ (Parental permission required)
Descript	Tool for audio/video editing, transcription, and AI voiceovers.	Free & Paid	13+ (Parental permission required)
D-ID	Specialises in generating videos featuring animated	Free & Paid	18+

	digital avatars		
EduAide AI	AI-powered platform for generating lesson plans, assessments, and rubrics, aimed at saving time for teachers.	Free & Paid	18+
Eleven Labs	Text-to-speech platform for generating realistic AI voices.	Free & Paid	13+ (Parental permission required)
Gamma	AI-powered presentation tool for generating slides from prompts.	Free	13+ (Parental permission required)
Gemini (Google)	Google's AI model for conversational and search applications.	Free & Paid	13+ (Parental permission required)
Goblin.tools	Goblin.tools is a collection of AI-powered tools designed to simplify daily tasks. Includes a formaliser tools, great for supporting with emails. etc.	Free & Patreon	13+ (Parental permission required)
HeyGen	AI tool for creating videos using avatars from text prompts.	Free	13+ (Parental permission required)
Ideogram	Designed for generating images from text. Has good text rendering	Free & Paid	13+ (Parental permission required)

	capabilities.		
Khanmigo (Khan Academy)	AI tutor designed to enhance personalised learning for students.	Free	13+ (Parental permission required)
Llama (Meta)	Meta's language model designed for advanced text generation.	N/A Currently banned in the EU. VPN Required to access	18+
Magicschool.ai	AI tools to help teachers create lesson plans and educational content.	Free & Paid	18+
MidJourney	AI art generator that creates detailed and visually stunning images from text.	Paid	13+ (Parental permission required)
Mindjoy	AI platform focused on STEM education with AI tutors and lesson planning tools.	Free	13+ (Parental permission required)
Mizou	AI-powered platform for creating chatbots tailored to tutoring, assessing, and grading students.	Free	18+ (but any chatbots can be shared students)
New Arc	A AI tool that converts sketches or images into realistic, high-quality renderings.	Free Education Licences	No ages restrictions in education license Terms and Conditions. I

			would recommend ages 7+
NotebookLM (Google)	AI-powered research and note-taking tool that summarises and generates insights from your documents.	Free	18+ (but any chatbots can be shared students)
Notion AI	AI extension for Notion for task management, note-taking, and content creation.	Paid	18+
Otter.ai	Transcription tool for meetings and interviews.	Free & Paid	13+ (Parental permission required)
Perplexity	AI-powered search engine for generating concise and direct answers.	Free	13+ (Parental permission required)
Pi (Inflection AI)	Emotional AI chatbot designed for engaging conversations.	Free	18+
Poe AI	An AI platform that hosts multiple models like GPT-4, Claude, and Llama, allowing users to interact with various AI chatbots. Poe enables users to create and monetize custom bots.	Free & Paid	18+ (but any chatbots and be shared students)

Quizizz	Quiz-based learning platform with gamified assessments. Has AI tools to support quiz creation and planning.	Free	13+ (Parental permission required)
Replika	AI chatbot for companionship and mental health support.	Free & Paid	13+ (Parental permission required)
Runway	AI video generation and editing platform.	Free & Paid	13+ (Parental permission required)
sAInaptic	AI-driven platform for automating the marking process and providing personalised feedback.	Free Trial & Paid	18+
SchoolAI	AI platform that helps teachers, students, and administrators by generating personalised learning tools, lesson plans, and feedback.	Free & Paid	18+
Speechify	Text-to-speech tool for turning written content into spoken audio.	Free & Paid	13+ (Parental permission required)
TeacherMatic	AI tool that helps teachers create lesson plans, quizzes, and assessments, with tools for simplifying lesson preparation.	Free	18+

TeachMateAI	AI-powered platform designed to assist teachers with tasks such as lesson planning, report writing, and assessments.	Free	18+
ThingLink + Blockade Labs	An interactive media platform that allows users to add rich, interactive elements to images, videos, and 360°/VR content. Now, through a partnership with Blockade Labs, you can use AI to create immersive VR environments.	Paid	Students and teachers can have accounts.
Tome	AI-powered storytelling tool for creating engaging presentations.	Free & Paid	13+ (Parental permission required)